Bog Mummies:
Preserved in Peat

by Charlotte Wilcox

Consultant:

Arthur C. Aufderheide, M.D.

Professor of Pathology

University of Minnesota, Duluth

CAPSTONE
HIGH-INTEREST
BOOKS

an imprint of Capstone Press
Mankato, Minnesota

Capstone High-Interest Books are published by Capstone Press
151 Good Counsel Drive, P.O. Box 669, Mankato, Minnesota 56002
http://www.capstone-press.com

Library of Congress Cataloging-in-Publication Data
Wilcox, Charlotte.
    Bog mummies: preserved in peat/by Charlotte Wilcox.
    p. cm.—(Mummies)
    Summary: Describes bog mummies, some of the most famous bog mummies and
where they have been found, how bogs create mummies, how scientists study them,
and what they can teach us about the past.
    Includes bibliographical references and index.
    ISBN 0-7368-1306-3 (hardcover)
    1. Lindow Man—Juvenile literature. 2. Bog bodies—Juvenile literature.
[1. Lindow Man. 2. Bog bodies. 3. Human remains (Archaeology) 4. England—
Antiquities.] I. Title. II. Series.
GN780.22.G7 W53 2003
569.9—dc21   2001007933

Editorial Credits
Carrie Braulick, editor; Karen Risch, product planning editor; Kia Adams, designer;
    Jo Miller, photo researcher

Photo Credits
Bettmann/CORBIS, 19
Chris Lisle/CORBIS, cover
© Copyright The British Museum, 6
David Muench/CORBIS, 15
Ecoscene/CORBIS, 12
Michael S. Yamashita/CORBIS, 29
Hulton Archive by Getty Images, 4
Moesgard Museum, 20
National Museum of Denmark, 23
Silkeborg Museum, Denmark, 16, 28
Stiftung Schleswig-Holsteinische Landesmuseen Schloss Gottorf, Germany, 10,
    24, 26

Table of Contents

Features

Learn About:

- The Lindow mummies
- Bog mummies of Europe
- Ancient mummy discoveries

Peat bog workers discovered Lindow I in 1983.

Chapter One

Lindow Moss Discoveries

Andy Mould and Eddie Slack worked in a peat bog called Lindow Moss in northwestern England. They loaded chunks of the heavy, dark peat onto an elevator. The soil went to a plant that made fuel. In the past, many Europeans used fuel made from peat to heat their homes.

On May 13, 1983, Andy saw an object on the elevator. It was flat, brown, and leathery. The plant manager looked at the object. He thought it was an old soccer ball.

An archaeologist discovered
Lindow II in 1984.

The workers washed the object to see it clearly. An eyeball and hair then appeared. The leathery object was a human head.

Scientists studied the head. They believed it was thousands of years old. Scientists named the head Lindow I.

More Shocking Discoveries

In summer 1984, Andy and Eddie were loading peat again. Andy saw an object he thought was a piece of wood. He threw it toward Eddie. The object dropped to the ground. They then saw that it was part of a human leg.

An archaeologist came to the bog. These scientists study ancient objects. The archaeologist found the top half of a body buried in the peat. Scientists estimated the body was about 2,000 years old. They named this body Lindow II.

Lindow Moss became famous for its bog mummies. Workers found another body in 1987. Scientists named it Lindow III. This body did not have a head. Some scientists believe the Lindow I head belongs to the Lindow III body.

Major Bog Mummy Discoveries

NORTHERN EUROPE

ATLANTIC OCEAN

Baltic Sea

DENMARK

North Sea

IRELAND

ENGLAND   HOLLAND

GERMANY

EUROPE

N

W   E

S

Miles   200   400

Kilometers   200

Map Legend

● Areas where bog mummies
  have been found

The Bog Bodies of Europe

Discoveries such as those in Lindow Moss are common in Europe. As many as 2,000 bodies or body parts have been found in Europe's peat bogs.

People have found hundreds of mummies while cutting peat in Denmark and Germany. People also have discovered bog mummies in England, Ireland, and other parts of northwestern Europe.

Scientists believe most bog bodies are between 300 and 2,300 years old. Conditions in the peat bogs prevent the bodies from rotting.

Fears of the Walking Dead

Many bog mummies were covered with stones or pieces of wood. These objects pinned the mummies underwater.

Long ago, some Europeans believed criminals could come back to life after death. Some archaeologists believe some people who became bog mummies may have been criminals. They believe ancient Europeans may have placed objects over the bodies to prevent them from coming back.

- Mummy features
- Sphagnum moss
- Conditions in peat bogs

Well-preserved bog mummies may have skin, hair, and eyes.

Chapter Two

How Bogs Form Mummies

All living things decay after death. Small organisms called bacteria and fungi eat a dead body's tissues. The tissues break down until only a skeleton remains. But some bodies in peat bogs do not decay. Certain conditions in the bogs prevent bacteria and fungi from growing.

Bog mummies may have skin and eyes. They also may have organs such as the stomach or intestines. Some bodies are preserved so well that they look like they died recently.

Some peat bogs have a fen. Eventually, peat fills the fen.

How Bogs Form

Peat bogs form slowly. They begin as ponds or lakes. Over thousands of years, they lose water. Layers of dead plant material pile up on the bottom. Sphagnum moss grows on the surface. This plant easily absorbs water.

Layers of dead sphagnum pile on top of each other. Gradually, the layers pack together and turn into peat. Peat can be 10 to 40 feet (3 to 12 meters) thick.

A Cold Fen

A fen is an open water area on a bog's surface. A body must die in a fen or be placed in a fen soon after death to become a mummy. Peat then forms around the body.

The water in the bog must be cold to mummify a body. It needs to be nearly at a freezing temperature of 32 degrees Fahrenheit (0 degrees Celsius). The cold water slows the growth of bacteria and fungi.

Bog Brains

Archaeologists found 167 skeletons in a peat bog in Florida between 1982 and 1987. Scientists believe some of these skeletons may be more than 4,000 years old.

A few of the Floridian skulls had mummified brain tissue inside. The brains are the only mummified tissues ever found in a North American bog. These brain tissues still contain DNA. This chemical is in a person's cells. It determines a person's physical features.

DNA is rare in bog mummies. Peat usually destroys DNA. Scientists are testing the DNA to learn more about the skeletons in the bog.

Sphagnum Moss

Sphagnum moss releases chemicals that prevent bacteria and fungi from growing. Scientists disagree about how sphagnum preserves bodies. Some scientists believe sphagnum moss releases a substance when it dies. They believe the substance prevents the growth of bacteria and fungi in various ways. For example, they believe it traps the water's nitrogen. Bacteria and fungi need this gas to grow.

Some bog mummies are better preserved than others. Some partially decayed bodies may have been exposed to air before they were covered with water. Oxygen in air helps bacteria and fungi grow. Well-preserved mummies probably were in bog water at or soon after death.

Sphagnum moss does not only help keep bodies from decaying. Bodies covered in sphagnum moss become tanned. The bones become soft. The soft bones allow the peat's weight to flatten the bodies. Chemicals in the sphagnum cause both of these reactions to occur.

Sphagnum moss prevents the growth of bacteria and fungi.

Learn About:
- Tollund Man
- Scientific methods
- Results of scientific studies

Scientists believe the Tollund Man was hanged.

Chapter Three

Bog Mummy Secrets Revealed

Scientists sometimes can easily discover how mummies died. In 1950, farmers discovered a bog mummy in a region of central Denmark called Tollund Fen. Scientists called this mummy Tollund Man. A rope was coiled around his neck. They believe he was hanged. Scientists estimate that Tollund Man is more than 2,000 years old.

Other clues can help scientists discover how a person died. Some mummies have a crushed skull or a cut throat. But scientists try to learn more than just a person's cause of death. They try to learn as much as they can about the person's life.

Radiocarbon Dating

Scientists may use radiocarbon dating to find out a mummy's age. All organisms contain radiocarbon called carbon 14. This element slowly breaks down after the organism's death. Scientists believe ancient remains contain little carbon 14.

Scientists also can test objects made of animal or plant parts for carbon 14. For example, they may test a rope or a piece of leather buried in peat.

Radiocarbon dating can produce varied results. Tissue from Lindow II went to three laboratories. Researchers at each laboratory estimated a different age for the samples. Scientists from one lab said Lindow II was 1,500 years old. Researchers at another lab

Scientists carefully studied Lindow II to learn about his health, diet, and cause of death.

said the mummy was 2,000 years old. The third laboratory's researchers tested the peat that surrounded Lindow II. They believed the peat was about 2,400 years old.

Studying Teeth

Scientists often use x-ray machines to view mummies' teeth. These machines take pictures of the inside of a body. Scientists could damage a mummy by opening its mouth to study the teeth.

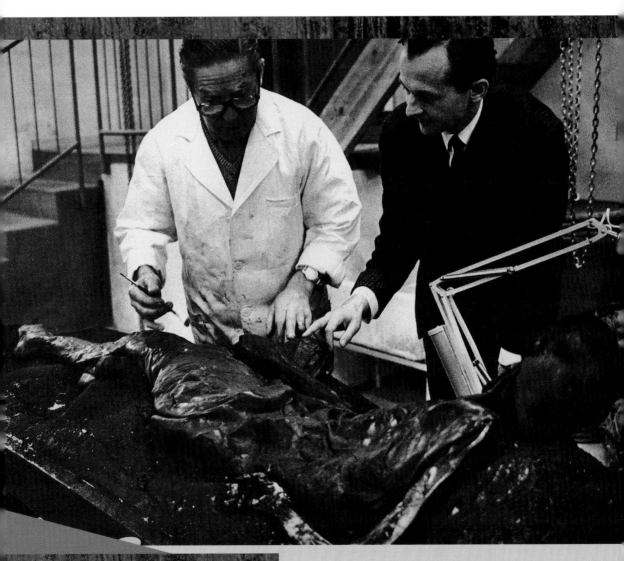

Bog workers discovered Grauballe Man in 1952.

Today, most people have tooth fillings. Dentists place these substances in decayed teeth. A lack of fillings is a clue that a mummy may be from ancient times. X-rays of Lindow II showed a full set of teeth but no fillings. This fact supports the scientists' beliefs that the person lived in ancient times.

Mummies under a Microscope

In 1952, peat bog workers in Denmark found a mummy. Scientists named the mummy Grauballe Man. They placed tissue from his stomach and intestines under a microscope to view it closely. The scientists discovered that Grauballe Man ate cooked cereal and meat shortly before he died. They also found parasites in Grauballe Man's intestines. These small organisms live on or inside people or animals.

Scientists have studied tissue samples from other bog mummies. They discovered that many of these mummies had no fresh fruits or vegetables in their stomachs. Their stomachs contained only grains and seeds. This fact leads scientists to believe that the people died during winter or early spring.

Mummy Hands

Mummies' hands also can provide scientists with clues. The Lindow mummies had smooth hands with neatly trimmed nails. Tollund Man, Grauballe Man, and Denmark bog mummy Borremose I also had smooth hands. These people probably did not grow crops or fight in battles. Scientists believe they may have been community or religious leaders.

Trephination

At least three skulls from peat bogs in Denmark show signs of trephination. People who performed this ancient operation cut a hole in a person's head. They then removed a small round or square-shaped piece of bone from the skull.

Trephination was a common practice throughout the world in ancient times. Scientists believe people in ancient times had doctors called medicine men. Scientists think medicine men may have used trephination to try to cure illnesses. Some scientists also believe people may have performed trephination on dead bodies. These people may have taken out pieces of bone to make charms.

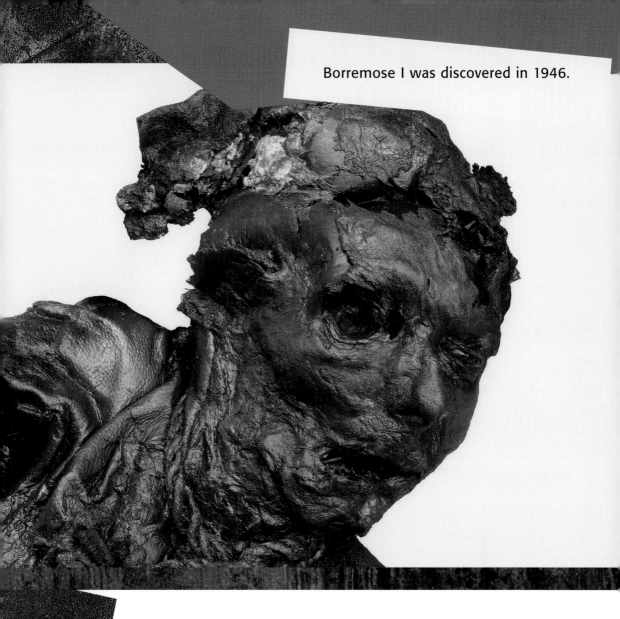

The skin of Grauballe Man's hands was so well preserved that police were able to take his fingerprints. The fingerprints displayed a pattern that is still common among Danish people today.

Mysteries remain about how people who became bog mummies died.

Chapter Four

Bog Mummy Mysteries

Bog mummies fascinate many people. They wonder how those who became bog mummies died. One of the greatest puzzles about bog mummies is why they are in a bog.

Scientists have different opinions about these mysteries. Some people who became bog mummies may have killed themselves. Others may have been criminals. People may have hanged these criminals and thrown their bodies into a fen. Some people may have drowned after they fell into a fen.

In 1952, the Windeby Girl was discovered in Germany. She was blindfolded and one side of her head was shaved.

Pleasing the Spirits

Scientists believe many bog mummies were victims of human sacrifice. Many ancient people honored spirits. Some of these people believed human sacrifices pleased the spirits.

Some bog mummies have signs that suggest they were sacrificed. Many have marks around their necks. These people may have been choked or hanged. Other mummies have bruises and cuts. These people may have been beaten or stabbed.

Several Wounds

Some clues suggest death occurred after the people suffered more than one wound. It appears someone slammed an ax into the back of Lindow II's neck. A powerful hit from behind broke his neck and cracked open his skull. He also was choked and his throat was cut.

Lindow II's wounds fit the beliefs of some ancient Europeans. These people believed in three spirits. They thought they needed a human sacrifice for each spirit and that each spirit required a different type of killing.

Ancient Rituals

Evidence shows that sacrifices usually occurred in early spring at the top of a hill. Scientists believe community leaders may have cooked bread over a fire and broke it in pieces. They took one piece of bread and burned it black. They put all the pieces in a bag. Everyone picked a piece out of the bag. The person who chose the burned piece became the sacrifice victim.

Scientists believe Lindow II may have chosen the burned piece. Researchers found something burned in his stomach.

Scientists believe few bog bodies will be discovered in the future.

The Future of Bog Mummies

No one knows exactly why most bog mummies ended up in bogs. But scientists believe people will find few bog mummies in the future. Today, few Europeans heat their homes with fuel made from peat. Farmers drain peat bogs to turn them into farmland. Government officials in Holland and Denmark no longer allow people to cut peat. They want to protect the remaining bogs.

A few European companies still cut peat. But workers usually use modern machinery. In the past, people cut peat by hand. They worked close to the ground. Workers who use modern machinery are high above the ground. This position makes it harder for workers to see mummies.

Peat bog workers found the last bog mummy in 1987. This mummy was Lindow III. Today's scientists try to improve their study methods and invent new tools. These efforts can help existing mummies provide new knowledge about the past.

People cut peat by hand in the past.

Words to Know

archaeologist (ar-kee-OL-uh-jist)—a person who studies old buildings and objects to learn about the past

bacteria (bak-TIHR-ee-uh)—very small organisms; bacteria eat the soft tissue of dead bodies.

fen (FEN)—an open area of water in a bog

fungi (FUHN-jye)—a type of organism that has no leaves, flowers, or roots

organism (OR-guh-niz-uhm)—a living plant or animal

parasite (PA-ruh-site)—a small organism that lives on or inside a person or animal

radiocarbon (ray-dee-oh-KAR-buhn)—a type of carbon that breaks down over time

sphagnum (SFAG-nuhm)—a type of moss that turns to peat when it dies

x-ray machine (EKS-ray muh-SHEEN)—a machine that takes pictures of the inside of a body

To Learn More

Buell, Janet. *Bog Bodies.* Time Travelers. Brookfield, Conn.: Twenty-first Century Books, 1997.

Deem, James M. *Bodies from the Bog.* Boston: Houghton Mifflin, 1998.

Wilcox, Charlotte. *Mummies, Bones, and Body Parts.* Minneapolis: Carolrhoda Books, 2000.

Places of Interest

The British Museum
Great Russell Street
London WC1B 3DG
England
The remains of the Lindow mummies are located here.

National Museum of Natural History
Smithsonian Institution
10th Street and Constitution Avenue NW
Washington, DC 20560

Silkeborg Museum
Horedgårdsvej 7
8600 Silkeborg
Denmark
Tollund Man is on exhibit in this museum.

Internet Sites

Index